The History of Money

By Dana Meachen Rau

Reading consultant: Susan Nations, M.Ed., author/literacy coach/consultant

Gareth Stevens
Publishing

Please visit our Web site www.garethstevens.com. For a free color catalog of all our high-quality books, call toll free 1-800-542-2595 or fax 1-877-542-2596.

Library of Congress Cataloging-in-Publication Data

Rau, Dana Meachen, 1971–
    The history of money / by Dana Meachen Rau.
        p. cm. — (Money and banks)
    Includes bibliographical references and index.
    ISBN: 978-1-4339-3381-3 (pbk.)
    ISBN: 978-1-4339-3382-0 (6-pack)
    ISBN: 978-1-4339-3380-6 (library binding)
————1. Money—History—Juvenile literature. I. Title. II. Series.
    HG221.5.R37   2005
    332.4'9—dc22   2005042886

New edition published 2010 by
Gareth Stevens Publishing
111 East 14th Street, Suite 349
New York, NY 10003

New text and images this edition copyright © 2010 Gareth Stevens Publishing

Original edition published 2006 by Weekly Reader® Books
An imprint of Gareth Stevens Publishing
Original edition text and images copyright © 2006 Gareth Stevens Publishing

Art direction: Haley Harasymiw, Tammy West
Page layout: Michael Flynn, Dave Kowalski
Editorial direction: Kerri O'Donnell, Barbara Kiely Miller

Photo credits: Cover, pp. 1, 4, 12, 14, 19 © Shutterstock.com; pp. 5, 9, 14, 15 © North Wind Picture Archives; p. 6 © Charles Napier/The Bridgeman Art Library/Getty Images; p. 7 © Nancy Carter/ North Wind Picture Archives; p. 8 © McGraw/Getty Images; pp. 10, 13 courtesy of American Numismatic Association's Money Museum, Colorado Springs, Colorado; pp. 11, 17, 18 Diane Laska-Swanke; p. 12 ARS/USDA; p. 16 courtesy of Foster Swanke.

Printed in the United States of America

CPSIA compliance information: Batch #WW10GS: For further information contact Gareth Stevens, New York, New York at 1-800-542-2595.

Table of Contents

Boldface words appear in the glossary.

Making a Trade

People use money to buy things every day. Buying is like trading. Trading means giving someone something they need. In return, they give you something you need. When you buy a book, you give the store clerk money. The clerk gives you the new book.

When you buy something, you must trade money for what you want.

4

Another word for trading is **bartering**. Long ago, people did not use money. They bartered with each other. Bartering helped people get what they needed.

Native Americans and settlers bartered with each other.
They traded animal furs, tools, clothes, and food.

Think about a fisherman who lived many years ago. What would he need to do his job? He would need a boat and a net. How do you think fishermen got the things they needed for fishing?

Fishermen have always needed the right equipment to catch fish.

Long ago, people used stones and rocks as tools. They also used rocks to grind corn.

Another person in the fisherman's **village** might be a toolmaker. The toolmaker would spend his day collecting wood and vines from trees or stones from the ground. He would use these things to make tools. Maybe he had a large family. They would need food to eat. How do you think the toolmaker got food to feed his family?

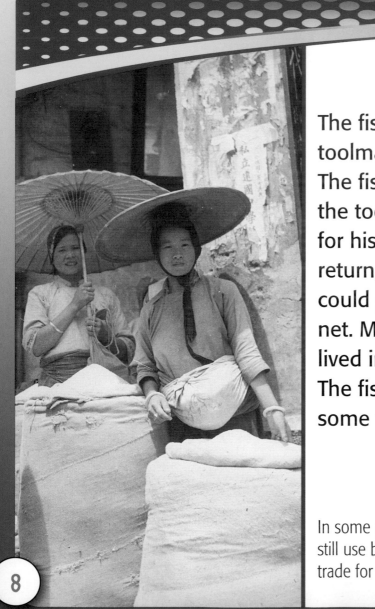

The fisherman and the toolmaker could barter. The fisherman could give the toolmaker some fish for his family to eat. In return, the toolmaker could give the fisherman a net. Maybe a boatbuilder lived in the village, too. The fisherman could trade some fish for a boat.

In some places, people still use bags of grain to trade for things they need.

So Many Kinds!

What if everyone in the village made the same thing? What if no one had the things other people needed? How could they barter for the things they needed? Bartering sometimes caused problems.

Sometimes, people had to decide if they wanted what others had to trade.

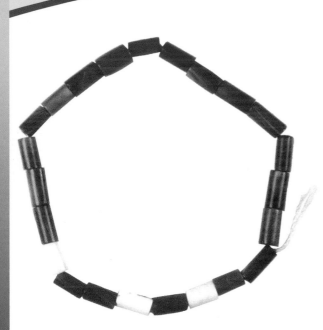

Native Americans put beads they called wampum on strings. Some early settlers used wampum as money when trading with Native Americans.

Money solved the problems. People decided to use one thing for money that everyone agreed was valuable to their community. Some people used cattle or animal furs. Other early forms of money included shells and seeds.

Seashells were one of the most common early forms of money. People in Africa, Thailand, and China used small seashells as money. The shells fit easily into their pockets. They were sometimes tied together on a string. People could carry the shells from village to village.

Small seashells like these are easy to carry.

In Mexico, people bought what they needed with **cacao** beans. They also used the beans to make a popular drink. Cacao beans are the main ingredient in chocolate.

Cacao beans grow inside the fruit of a cacao tree.
People in the past used the beans as money.

Coins and Paper

People began to travel to new lands and move to new places. Everyone agreed that gold, silver, and other **rare** metals were **valuable**. People started using metal as money.

This ancient Chinese money was made out of metal.
It was made in the shape of a key or a knife.

People all over the world made coins out of gold, silver, and other metals. They stamped pictures of kings, queens, gods, or animals on them. Some countries had holes in their coins. People could string the coins together to make them easier to count and carry. People in the land now called Turkey made the first coins about two to three thousand years ago.

Ancient Greek coins have pictures of faces and animals on them.

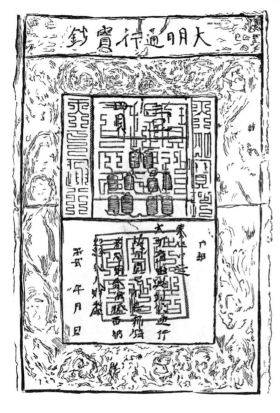

This early form of paper money is from China.

People wanted to keep their coins in a safe place. They left their coins with **merchants**. A merchant is a trader or someone who runs a store. The merchants gave people **receipts**. A receipt was a written piece of paper that showed the amount of money someone gave a merchant. People could spend the receipts like money at other stores. These receipts were the first paper money.

Today's Money

Today, people all over the world use different kinds of money. The type of money a country uses is called **currency**. Currency can be coins or paper money called bills.

Currency looks different all over the world.

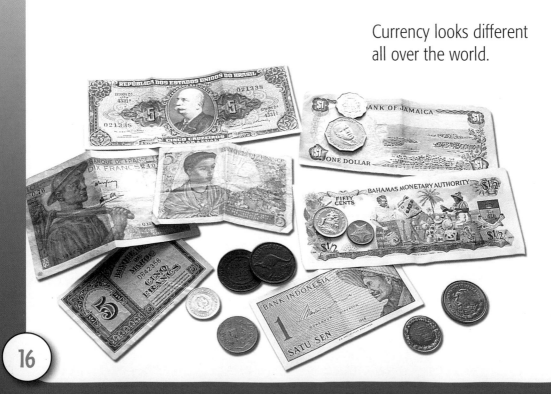

In the United States, people use dollars. The government makes all kinds of money. Paper money is made in many different dollar amounts. Coins equal parts of one dollar. Pictures of famous Americans from the past are on both paper money and coins.

The currency of the United States is the dollar.

Canada's currency is the Canadian dollar. In Mexico, people use pesos. Canadian and Mexican money has pictures of famous people from their histories, too. The money from these countries is very colorful. Their paper bills are blue, purple, red, green, and brown.

In Canada, the five-dollar bill has a picture of children playing hockey. In Mexico, the fifty peso bill has a picture of men fishing.

You can use both paper money and coins to buy a new toy or book. Both kinds of money fit in your pocket easily. It is much easier to use paper money and coins than a big bag of grain or a basket of fish!

The kind of money we use today makes shopping easy.

Math Connection: Count the Shells

Look at the graph below.
Use it to answer the questions on page 21.

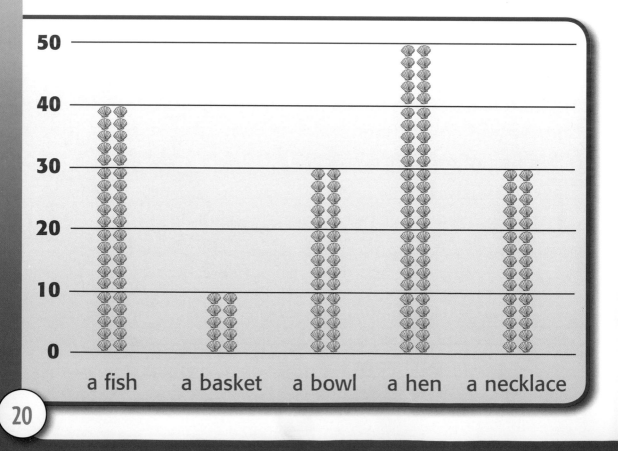

1. Which item costs the most shells to buy?

2. Which item costs the least?

3. Which items could you buy if you had thirty shells?

4. How many different items could you buy with one hundred shells?

Find the answers on page 23.

Glossary

bartering: trading one thing for another without using money

cacao: a tree that has seeds, or beans, which are used to make chocolate and cocoa

currency: the type of money that is used in a country

merchant: a person who runs a store; someone who buys and sells things

rare: not often found, seen, or happening

receipts: written slips of paper that show how much money has been paid and what has been bought

valuable: worth a lot of money

village: a community of people living together that is smaller than a town

For More Information

Books

Anderson, Jon Lee. *Smart About Money: A Rich History*. New York: Grosset & Dunlap, 2003.

Basel, Roberta. *The History of Money.* Mankato, MN: Capstone Press, 2006.

Haskins, Lori. *No Money? No Problem!* New York: Kane Press, 2004.

Web Sites

The History of Money
Library.thinkquest.org/28718/history.html
A simple timeline of money and how it has changed

Money Farm
wttw.com/moneyfarm/lessons/history.html
Lessons and quizzes about the history of money and other interesting money topics

Math Connection Answers: 1. a hen 2. a basket 3. a bowl or a necklace, or three baskets 4. three

Index

About the Author

Dana Meachen Rau is an author, editor, and illustrator. She has written more than one hundred books for children, including nonfiction, early readers, and historical fiction. She lives with her family in Burlington, Connecticut.